# TENOR
# SAXOPHONE
# Amazing Phrasing

## 50 WAYS TO IMPROVE YOUR IMPROVISATION SKILLS

### BY DENNIS TAYLOR

To access audio visit:
**www.halleonard.com/mylibrary**

6345-2057-7672-4963

ISBN 978-0-634-03540-1

7777 W. BLUEMOUND RD. P.O. BOX 13819 MILWAUKEE, WI 53213

Visit Hal Leonard Online at
**www.halleonard.com**

# Introduction

Good phrasing is essential to communicating musically. The exercises in this book teach the techniques behind phrasing and are designed to help you make the leap from playing notes to playing *music*.

This book is divided into sections on harmony, rhythm, and melody. Learning about these fundamental elements of music is just like learning a new language. At first you learn words—how they're spelled and pronounced. Next comes simple phrases and sentences, providing you with a basic understanding of the new words and how to use them. Eventually, you move into thinking and communicating in the new language.

The key to good phrasing is knowing when to play and when not to play. It's important to become your own editor. There's a famous story about Miles Davis and John Coltrane. During the *Kind of Blue* period in the late fifties, when they were playing modal compositions, Coltrane was having a hard time ending his solos because of the lack of a closing cadence. Davis wanted Coltrane to cut down on the length of his solos, and 'Trane replied that he didn't know how to get out of them. Miles' response was, "Just take the horn out of your mouth."

One important quality that all great musicians share is flexibility, both in sound (a large tonal palate) and meter (the ability to play behind the beat, in front of the beat, etc.), so they don't sound like machines. Versatility in these two areas will lead to good phrasing, the ability to express yourself, and originality of style.

## How to Use This Book

For a long time, I was reluctant to practice patterns. I thought it would make my playing more mechanical and predictable. But when I did start working with patterns, I discovered that just the opposite was true. My ear improved tremendously, allowing me to be more creative and expressive in my playing. Some of the patterns in this book are technique builders, and you will want to incorporate these into your daily practice regime. Others are for playing over specific chords, and you can use the online audio to hear how they work together. (You can remove the saxophone from the track by panning the balance knob all the way to the left.)

In working with these patterns, try to avoid writing them out. This will help develop your ear immeasurably. If the pattern is too long to remember, break it down into smaller segments. Work toward being able to sing the phrases through the transpositions—in other words, think in terms of phrases rather than thinking of every note and its relationship to the chord. If something in the pattern sparks in you a song or another pattern, go with it. You can always return to the original pattern. It's all part of being flexible and reacting to your musical environment. By improving the connection between your ear and your fingers, you will develop the confidence and the ability to play whatever you hear.

On the études that have audio accompaniment, the written solos are just a starting point. Once you're familiar with the written version, try your hand at writing your own renditions, incorporating certain ideas that you like from what's in the book. Then pan out the sax and play your written solos with the rhythm track. Finally, take your own improvised solos.

Have fun and enjoy the book.

# Contents

# Modes

*Idea #* 1

In classical music, the use of modes can be traced to twentieth-century composers like Ravel and Debussy. Looking for a new palate of tonal colors, they began exploring these permutations of basic Western scales. Named for Greek cities and regions, some modes—like the Ionian and Aeolian—are just other names for familiar scales like the major scale and natural minor scale. Other modes, like Dorian and Phrygian, are derived from folk music in other countries.

In jazz, modes played an important role in the "cool" school of bebop. As musicians grew tired of bebop's complex chord progressions and were looking for a fresh sound, they simplified the chords, often using one chord for many measures, and based the melodies and improvisations on new-sounding scales or modes. Miles Davis was at the vanguard of this new style, as documented on his 1959 masterpiece *Kind of Blue*. The new modes also seeped into popular music—the Mixolydian mode was used in the opening measures of the Beatles' tune "Norwegian Wood."

Our first example is an Ionian scale (major scale). Notice that the two half steps are between the third and fourth degrees, and the seventh and root.

**Ionian**

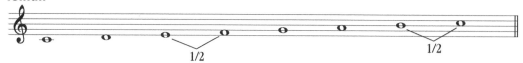

The Dorian mode is built on the second degree of a major scale. For example, D Dorian mode consists of the same notes as a C major scale. The Dorian mode may also be thought of as a major scale with a minor third and minor seventh, and it would naturally be used over a minor chord. The second, fourth, and sixth degrees provide the richest sonorities. Some tunes that are based on Dorian modes are "So What" (Miles Davis), "Impressions" (John Coltrane), and "Little Sunflower" (Freddie Hubbard).

**Dorian**

The Phrygian mode is built on the third degree of a major scale—e.g., from E to E using the notes from the C major scale. Notice the Spanish flavor of this scale. Use of the Phrygian is usually independent of a specific chord; the music would simply state Phrygian mode. Some compositions that utilize this mode are "Flamenco Sketches" (Miles Davis/Bill Evans), "Olé" (John Coltrane), and "Masqualero" (Wayne Shorter).

**Phrygian**

Lydian is a major-sounding mode and has the same notes as the major scale a fourth below; it's essentially a major scale with a raised fourth degree. This mode is usually played over a major chord, a major 7#11 chord, or a major 7♭5 chord. Some tunes based on this mode include "In Case You Haven't Heard" (Woody Shaw), "Black Narcissus" (Joe Henderson), and "Nefertiti" (Wayne Shorter).

## Lydian

Mixolydian mode is found on the fifth degree of the major scale and can be thought of as a major scale with a lowered seventh degree. The scale is applied to dominant seventh chords. Tunes that make use of the Mixolydian mode are "Maiden Voyage" and "Watermelon Man" (Herbie Hancock), "Well You Needn't" (Thelonious Monk), and "Killer Joe" (Benny Golson).

## Mixolydian

Aeolian mode is found on the sixth degree of the major scale. Also known as the natural minor, this scale is used over a minor chord when functioning as a tonic in a minor key. Some compositions that utilize the Aeolian mode are "My Favorite Things" (Richard Rodgers) and "Autumn Leaves" (Johnny Mercer).

## Aeolian

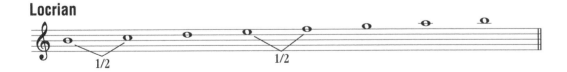

The Locrian mode is built on the seventh degree of the major scale. Its characteristic sound comes from the combination of a minor third, seventh, and sixth, plus a diminished interval between the root and the fifth. The Locrian mode is played over a minor 7♭5 chord, also known as a half-diminished chord. The minor 7♭5 chord usually functions as a II chord in a minor key. There are many compositions that utilize this mode, including "Airegin" (Sonny Rollins), "Night in Tunisia" (Dizzy Gillespie), "What Is This Thing Called Love," and "Night and Day" (Cole Porter).

## Locrian

# Major Scale Patterns

*Idea #*

The following major scale patterns are designed to improve technique and ear training as well as to combine aspects of harmony and phrasing that improvising musicians encounter on a regular basis. I recommend adopting the exercises as part of a daily warm-up routine. It wouldn't be practical to play each one in every key every day; work out a schedule based on your available time and level of playing that incorporates all of the patterns. The familiarity that comes from working on these every day will eventually allow you to focus on tone, attack, releases, and all the other subtleties that go into amazing phrasing. To develop your musical reflexes, it's best to transpose these exercises by ear.

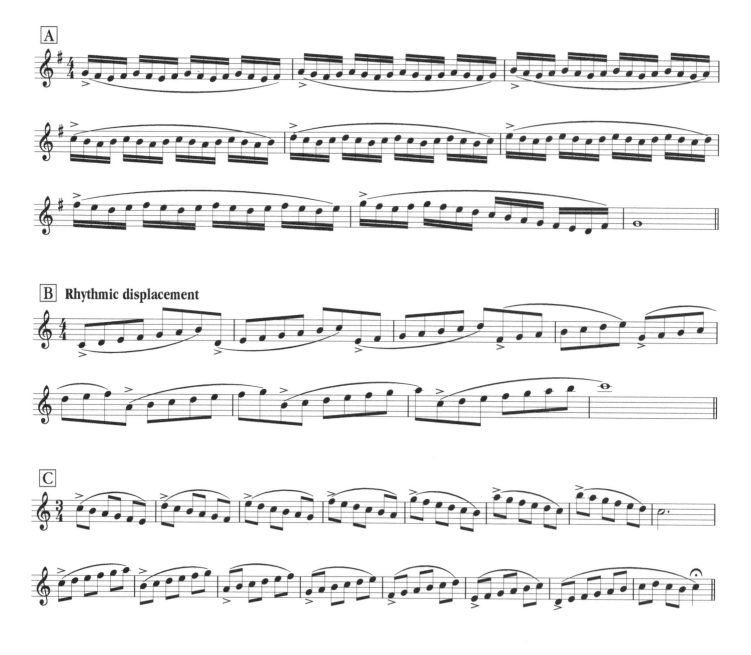

# Major Chord Patterns

## Idea #3

This series of patterns is based on major triads and major seventh chords. These exercises are designed to improve your technique and phrasing while also developing your ear. It's important to try playing these patterns through all the keys without writing them out. Make them a part of your daily practice routine. Practice using various tempos and articulations.

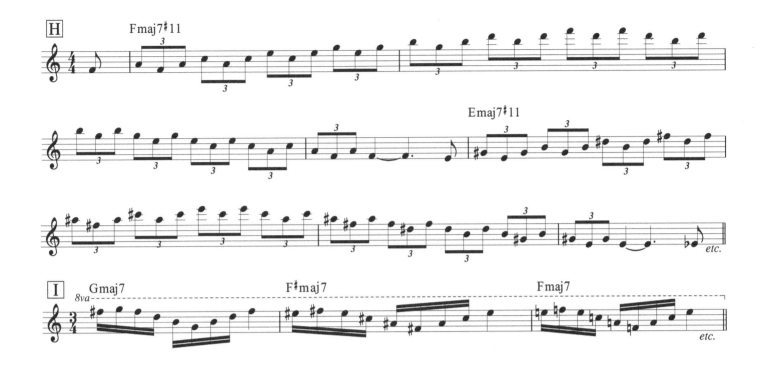

# Minor Chord Patterns

*Idea #*

These patterns are based on minor triads and minor seventh chords and are the minor-key equivalent of the patterns in Idea #3. Again, play through these patterns in all the keys without writing them out, and incorporate them into your daily practicing.

A  **Chromatic**

B  **Whole steps**

C  **Minor 7th chords**

D  **Minor (major 7)**

E  **Chromatic down**

F  **With major 7th**

G  **Minor 9th arpeggio**

H **Minor 9th arpeggio**

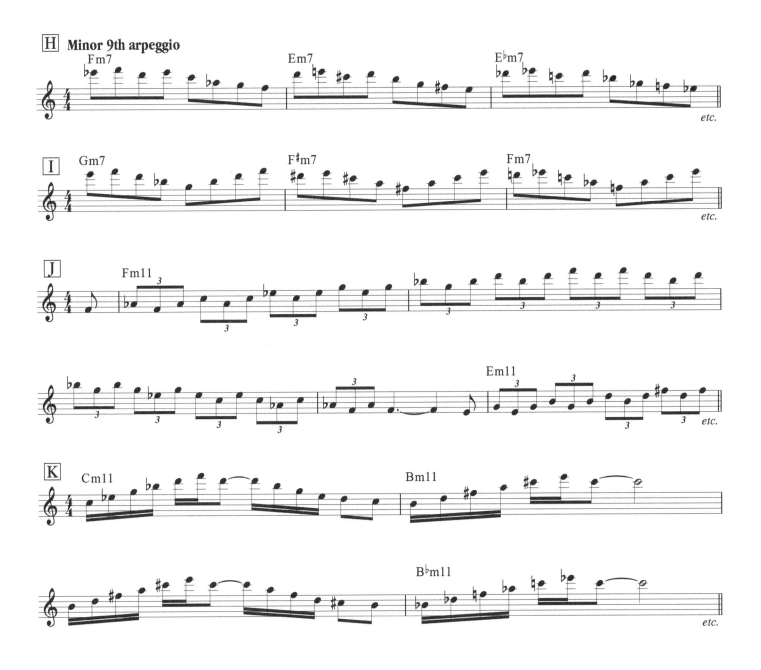

# Diatonic Seventh Chords

*Idea #*

In this exercise, we take the major scale and build a seventh chord on each pitch. Below, we start with the key of G and then move to F. Note that in every major scale, when you build a seventh chord on the I it will always be a major seventh, II is always minor, III is minor, IV is major, V is dominant, VI is minor, and VII is minor 7♭5. Repeat each exercise in all twelve keys.

**Key of G**

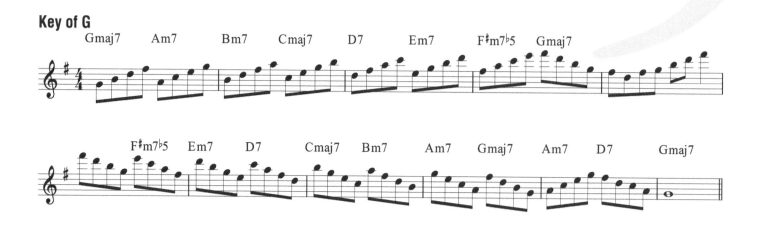

**Key of F**

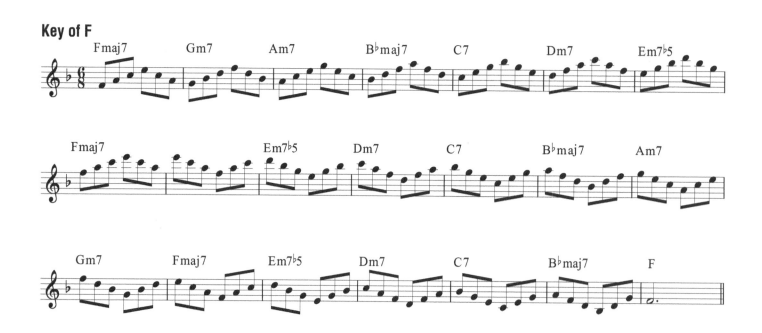

# Arpeggios

*Idea #*6

This exercise is designed to illustrate the five basic chord types—major, dominant, minor, minor 7♭5, and diminished. Starting with the major chord and changing one note at a time, work through the chords. After playing the arpeggios for a while, try singing them as an aid to developing your ear. Also familiarize yourself with the following chord symbols, which are commonly found in a fake book or lead sheet.

| | | | |
|---|---|---|---|
| *Major* | △ | M | MA |
| *Dominant* | 7 | dom7 | |
| *Minor* | −7 | m7 | mi7 |
| *Minor 7♭5* | −7♭5 | ø | |
| *Diminished* | ° | dim | |

Example A is in one octave. Example B is in two octaves (when applicable). Example C is in first inversion (starting on the third degree). Example D is in second inversion (starting on the fifth), and Example E is in third inversion (starting on the seventh).

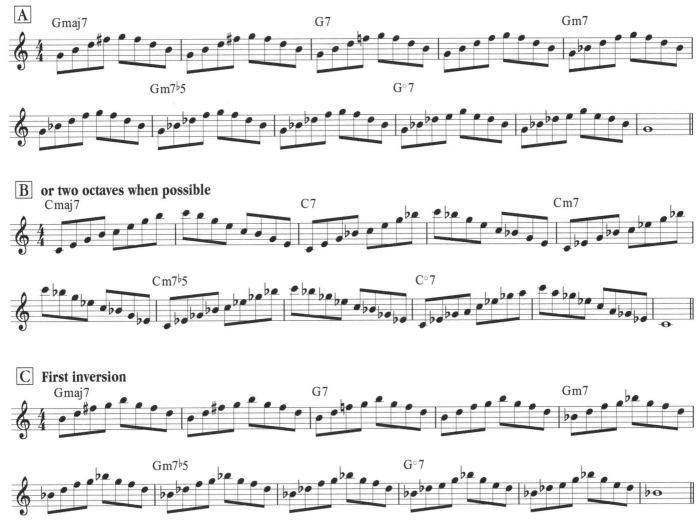

# Dorian Mode

*Idea #*

In Idea #1, we learned how to construct and play seven modes. Now let's try playing in the Dorian mode over this 32-measure progression. On the recording, you'll find accompaniment parts to play over.

First, play the Dorian scale through the chord changes.

**D Dorian**

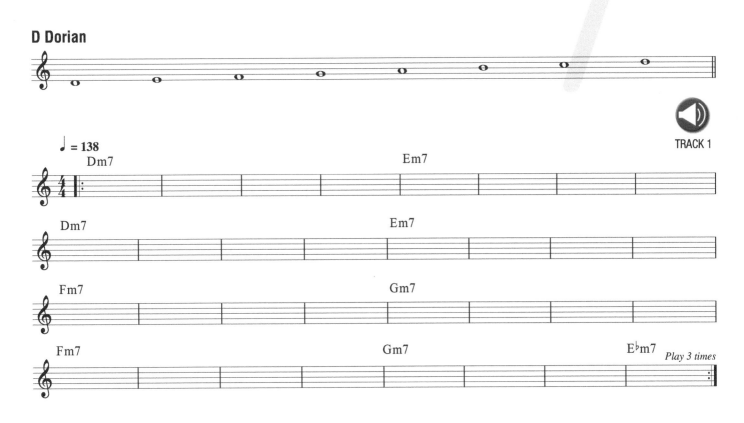

TRACK 1

Once you feel comfortable, try stretching and taking a solo using Dorian scales. Begin the phrases on an upbeat to give your lines momentum. Experiment with anticipating the chord change by a beat or two, as in the following example. This will help lead you into the next chord and give your phrases more direction.

# Mixolydian Mode

*Idea #*

As we saw in Idea #1, the Mixolydian scale is built off the fifth degree of a major scale (or you can think of it as a major scale with a lowered seventh degree). Here it is in C.

**C Mixolydian**

This scale is used on unaltered dominant seventh chords. Practice it with the chord progression on the recording, which is made up of dominant sevenths in the cycle of fourths.

TRACK 2

Finally, work on playing these patterns with the rhythm section on the recording. Try transposing the patterns without writing them out. Transpose by numbers if you have difficulty, but work toward being able to play the patterns in all keys by just using your ear and singing the lines.

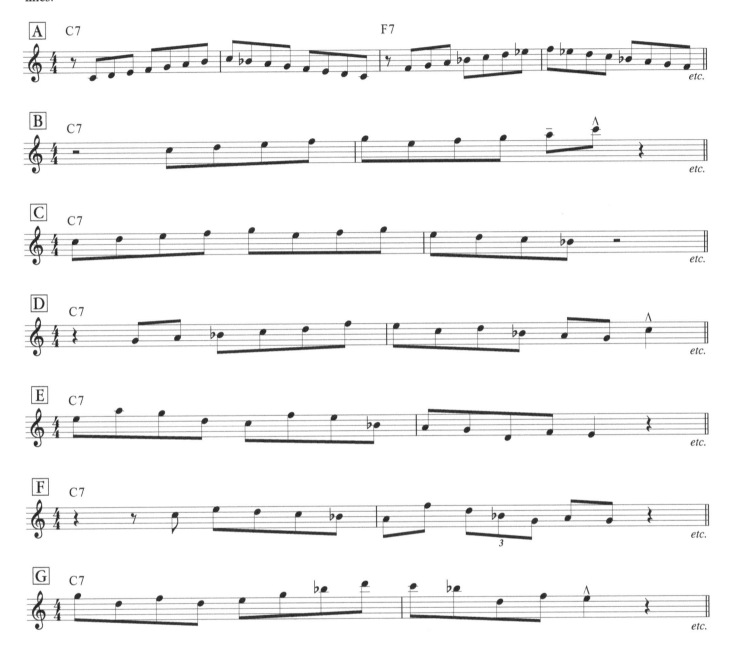

# *The II–V–I Progression*

*Idea #*

The II–V–I (or II7–V7–I) progression is the cornerstone of a great many compositions. Understanding these chords both aurally and technically will help you navigate many standard tunes, and recognizing these patterns will aid in your harmonic analysis. Each II–V–I signifies a key area or key of the moment. Grouping these chords into coherent phrases enables you to simplify what might at first glance seem to be a very complex chord progression. Looking at the big picture will smooth out your phrases and get you away from thinking from chord to chord.

All the patterns below deal with the Dorian, Mixolydian, and Ionian scales. They're designed to help you hear the progression as well as learn to play in all twelve keys. Examples involving alterations on the dominant seventh chords appear later in the book.

Practice these patterns along with this progression on the recording.

TRACK 3

# The Minor II–V–I

*Idea #*

**10**

Now let's look at the II–V–I progression in a minor key. The Locrian scale is used on the
IIm7♭5 chord except in Example I, which uses the Super Locrian scale (a raised ninth degree).
On the dominant seventh chords, a variety of ♯9 and ♭9 extensions are played. On
the I minor chord, the melodic minor, Dorian, or minor pentatonic scale is used.

Practice along with this progression on the recording.

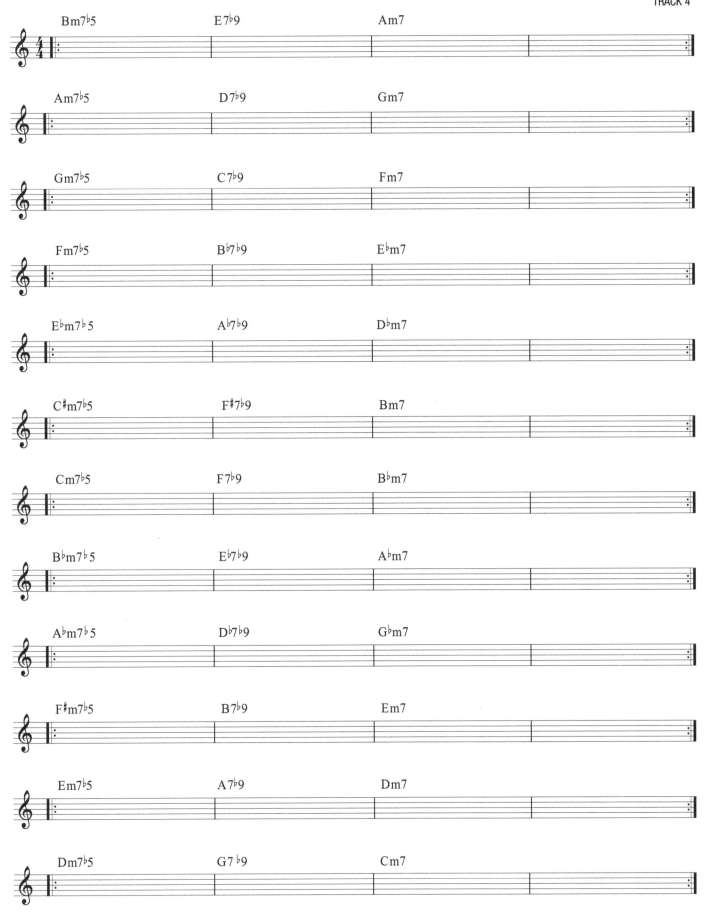

# IIm7-V7 Etude

## Idea # 11

Here is a twenty-four-measure étude running through a IIm7–V7–I7 chord progression in every key. You may play the étude as written or transpose each two-measure pattern throughout.

TRACK 5

Now try these six additional two-measure patterns in all twelve keys. These patterns add alterations to the upper extensions of the V7 chord (#9, ♭9, ♭5, etc.). Take them slowly and play each two-measure pattern without writing it out. Learn to trust your ear. As you become familiar with the progression, create your own two-measure patterns.

**Other Patterns**

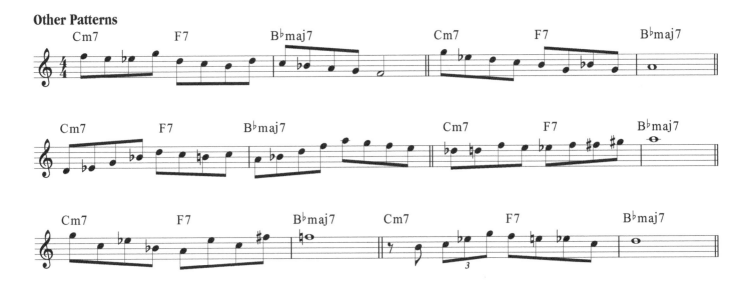

The next exercise runs through II–V moves in minor keys. For the tonic minor (Im7), the melodic minor or Dorian scale are the best choices. For the IIm7♭5, use the Locrian scale (seventh degree of a major scale). In a minor II–V progression, the V chord usually features a ♭9 alteration (the ♭5 of the II chord is the same note as the ♭9 of the V chord). Again, this exercise can be played as written or you can transpose and play each two-measure fragment through each chord change.

TRACK 6

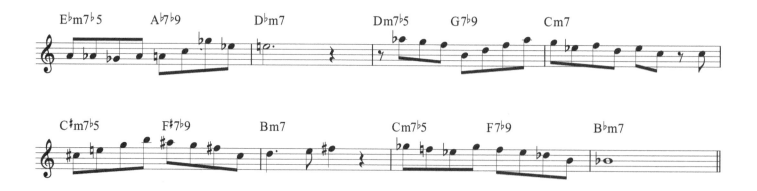

Finally, here are eight additional minor-key patterns. Pay special attention to patterns D, E, and G—they are based on the Super Locrian scale (Locrian scale with raised ninth).

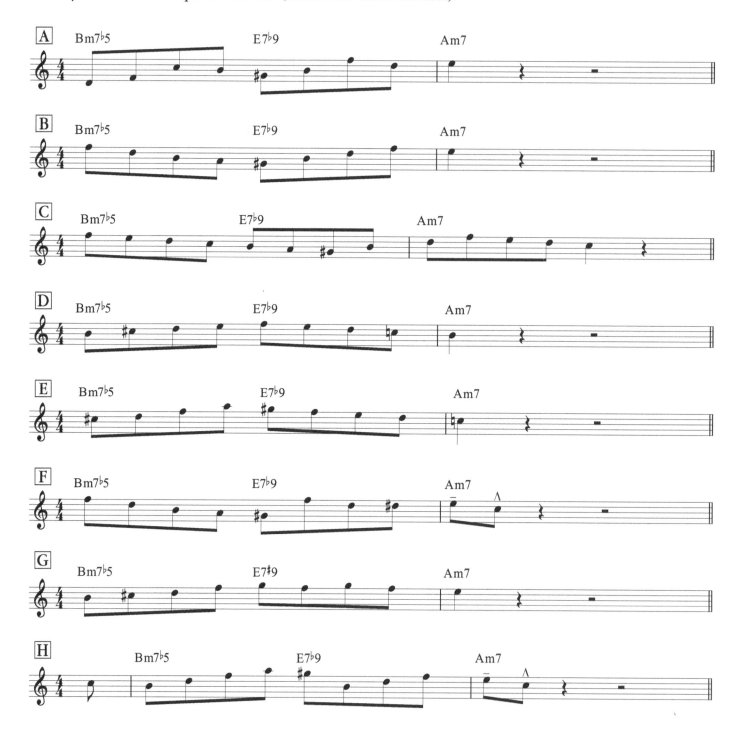

# One-Measure IIm7–V7 Patterns

*Idea #* 12

Continuing along the lines of idea #11, here are some one-measure IIm7–V7 patterns, first in major keys.

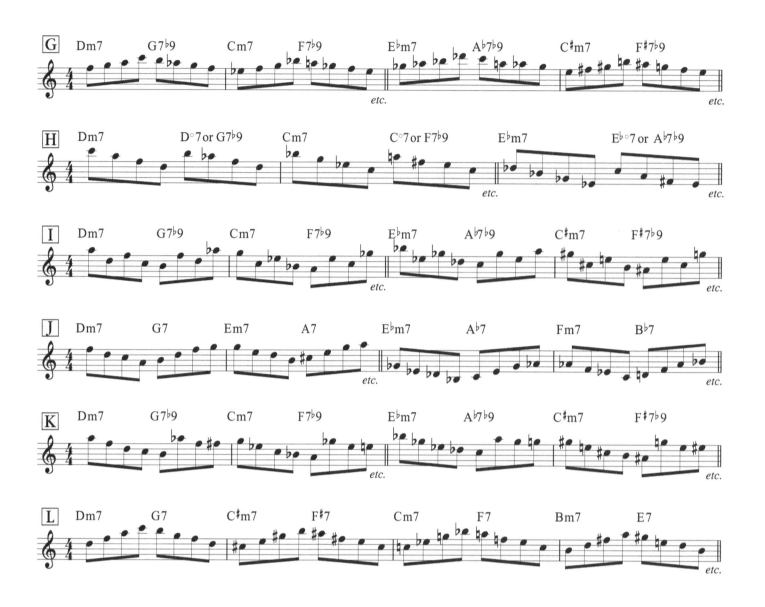

And now in minor keys. Also practice these patterns descending and ascending in whole steps.

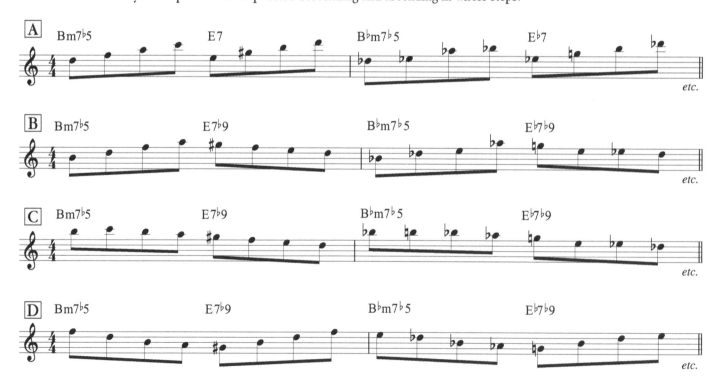

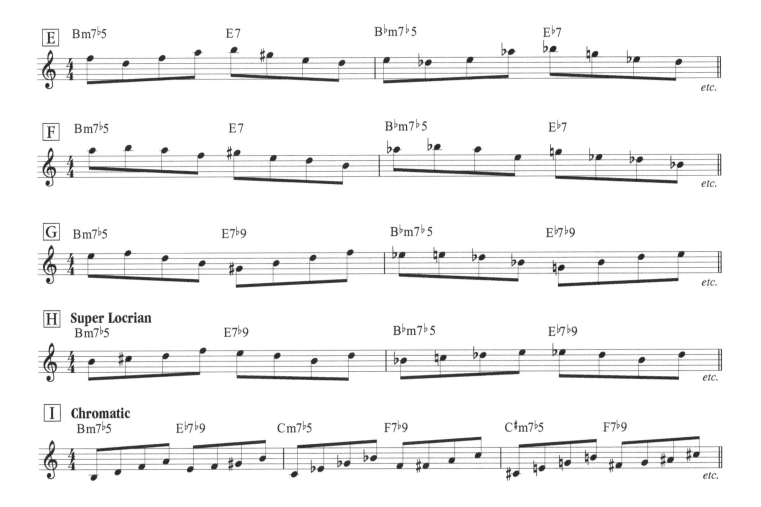

# Descending Ninth Chords

*Idea #*13

One of the best ways to train your ear to hear intervals and their relationship to chords is to play arpeggios through a chord progression. Many of the previous arpeggio exercises were root-based formations. In this exercise, we will concentrate on hearing an arpeggio played from the ninth of the chord down, in order to try and get beyond the up/down patterns usually associated with arpeggios. By starting on an extension, we are training the ear to hear the important color tone of the ninth.

When you're playing a repetitive pattern like this, try to make it sound like a piece of music rather than a musical drill. Paying close attention to the articulations and making it swing will help it come to life.

TRACK 7

# Fourths

Modern improvisers like Joe Farrell, David Liebman, and Eddie Harris often incorporate the interval of a fourth into their solos. The open or ambiguous sound of fourths allow the soloist to get away from the traditional sound of chords built in thirds. The following exercises will help train your ear to hear the interval as well as get the notes under your fingers.

Note that when playing in the diatonic scale, as in Example A, not every interval is a perfect fourth. The distance between the fourth and the seventh degrees is an augmented fourth. Play this exercise in all twelve keys.

The remaining exercises should be practiced with various articulations and tempos to help improve your phrasing.

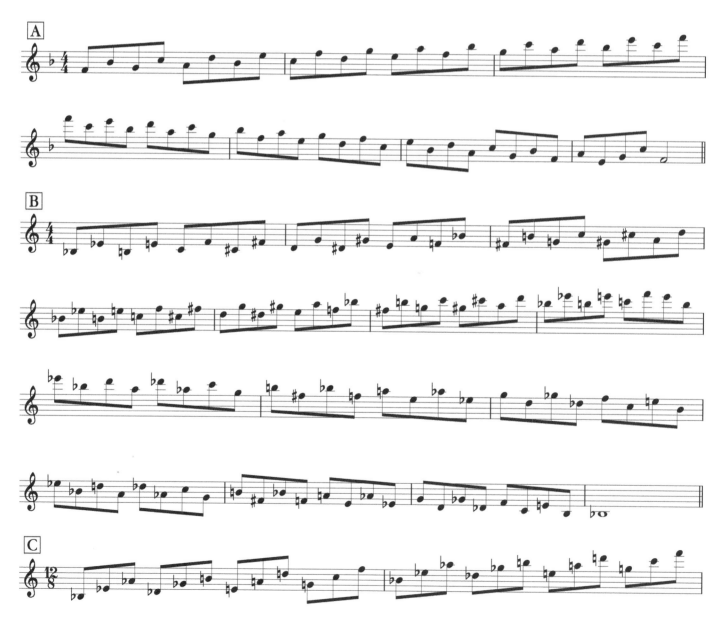

# Bebop Mixolydian

*Idea #*

One of the scales that came out of the bebop era of the forties was the bebop Mixolydian—an eight-note scale that features an added half step between the root and the lowered seventh. Many of the fast phrases in bebop featured a scalar approach, and the additional note makes the scale symmetrical and facilitates playing in bebop's quick tempos.

The bebop Mixolydian scale can be used on dominant seventh chords or on an entire II–V progression. Play all these patterns with track 2.

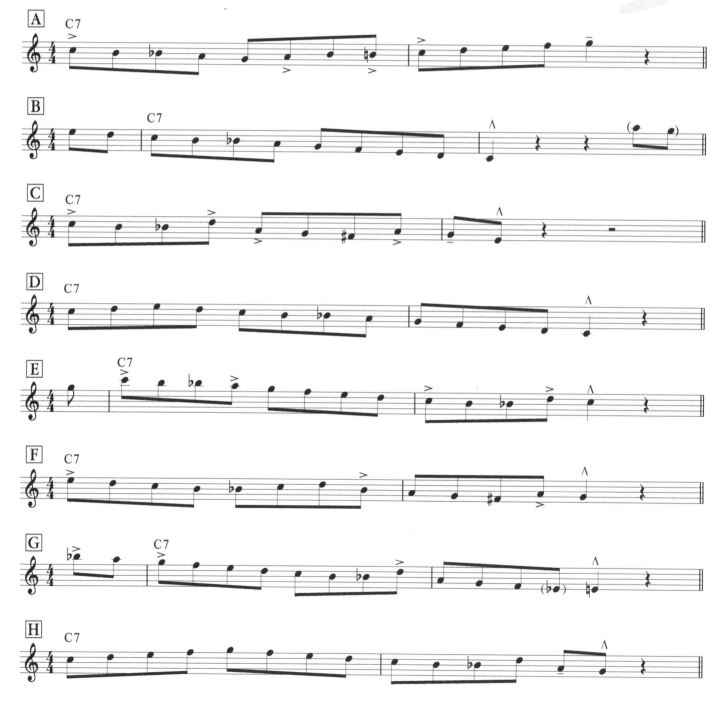

Play these patterns with track 3.

# The Diminished Scale

*Idea #* 16

The diminished scale is an eight-note symmetrical scale based on alternating whole steps and half steps (or half steps and whole steps). The scale gets its name from the diminished seventh chord, which is built by stacking minor thirds on top of each other (for example, G–B♭–D♭–E). Because of its symmetry, all inversions of the diminished chord have the same structure. Any of the four notes could be the root, and the only way to find the root is to analyze the spelling of the chord.

The ambiguous sound of the diminished scale makes it a popular tool for improvisers, who use it to alter a chord's upper extensions. This is the diminished whole-step/half-step scale used for improvising over a diminished chord.

*Diminished whole-step scale*

Use this half-step/whole-step diminished scale when you're improvising over a dominant seventh chord. The notes in the scale give the "color" tones of ♭9, ♯9, and ♭5. The scale should only be used on dominant chords when they possess a V–I relationship.

*Diminished half-step scale*

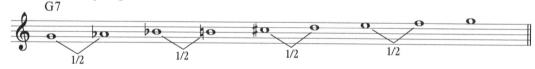

The next example shows the three diminished scales and the corresponding chords. Play them slowly with the metronome. After becoming comfortable with the scales, mentally recall the corresponding chord name and play the appropriate diminished scale from the chord's root to the highest note on your horn in that scale, and then back down to the root.

| B♭Y7 | D♭Y7 | EY7 | GY7 | whole-step scale |
| C7 | E♭7 | G♭7 | A7 | half-step scale |

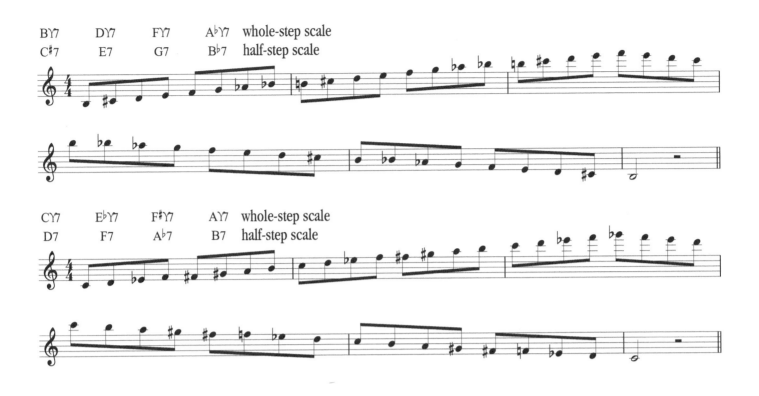

Here is a common diminished scale pattern and the corresponding diminished and dominant seventh chords.

Now let's look at nine different diminished scale patterns you can practice with track 8 (altered dominants). Try working them out slowly. Some of these patterns may be too long at first and may be easier to work with by breaking them down into smaller segments.

Try transposing each pattern to C7.

The final exercise features more diminished scale patterns—this time over II–V–I chords.
Practice them with track 3.

# The Altered Scale

Through the use of the altered extension, improvisers can increase the amount of tension in their lines. There are many scales that alter one or more extensions, but the altered scale alters all the extensions (♭9, ♯9, ♯11, and ♭13). The altered scale is based on the jazz melodic minor scale—a minor scale with a raised sixth and seventh both ascending and descending. This differs from the traditional melodic minor, which lowers the seventh and sixth degrees when descending.

*G Jazz Melodic Minor*

The augmented major chord built off the third is what gives this scale its unique sound.

*Augmented Major 7th*

To find the altered scale for a dominant seventh chord, build a jazz melodic minor scale a half step above the root.

The altered scale works best when the dominant seventh chord has a V–I root movement. This scale can be used on V7 chords that have the abbreviation *alt* next to them or on chords that have only some of the extensions altered, like a V7♭9 or a V7♯9. By building an augmented major seventh chord off of the third, you can get the ♯9 and ♭13 extensions (see Example A). Building an augmented major 7th chord from the ♭7 gives you the ♯11 alteration (Example B). The jazz melodic minor will also work on half-diminished chords if you build the scale off of the third of the chord (Examples J to O).

[A] **C♯ Jazz Melodic Minor**

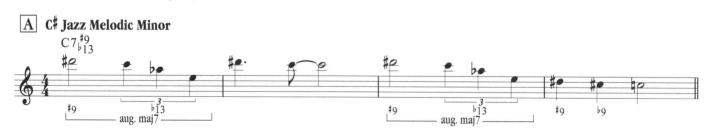

Examples A, B, and C can be played with the altered dominant progression below. Examples D through H can be played with track 3 (IIm7–V7–I). Examples J through O should be played with track 4 (IIm7♭5–V7–Im).

**TRACK 8**

An experienced rhythm section will follow your lead if you begin altering chords. However, you can play altered scales over the appropriate dominant seventh chord whether or not the rhythm section alters the chord. In the following exercise, the rhythm section is playing basic voicings and you, the improvisor, are playing the alterations.

Practice these patterns with Track 2, then try your hand at creating your own patterns.

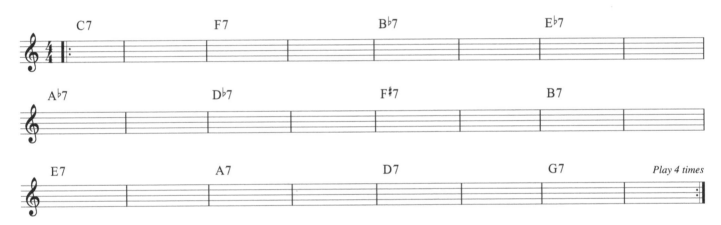

# *The Whole-Tone Scale*

*Idea #* 18

Like its name suggests, the whole-tone scale is made up entirely of notes a whole step apart. This gives the scale a very identifiable and exotic sound. Because of the relationship of intervals, the melodic possibilities are somewhat limited.

The whole-tone scale is best used when improvising over augmented triads or dominant seventh chords with either a raised or lowered fifth and a major ninth.

Due to their symmetry, there are only two possible whole-tone scales. Practice the following whole-tone scales with track 8.

*etc.*

*etc.,*

# Polychords

*Idea #*

19

Stacking one triad over another chord creates a polychord. In the first example below, the piano is sounding a concert B♭7 chord. The saxophone begins within the sound of the chord with a concert B♭ triad, then extends that into a C concert triad, forming a #11 chord.

The polychord creates an interesting tonal color. There are five major triads and six minor triads that can be used. The V minor and VI minor triads do not give any upper structure alterations. Studying the polychord chart below will help you hone in on a specific alteration. If the chord change calls for a #9♭13 dominant 7 chord, playing a major triad off the ♭6 will give you just that. Using a diminished scale would give you the #9, but it would also give you a ♭9 and #11. The altered scale will give you all the alterations: ♭9, #9, #11, and ♭13.

To learn how these specific alterations work, look at the chart and listen to the sax and piano play the different polychords. Note the unique sound of each example. Then pan out the sax on the audio and experiment with playing different polychords, always being aware of what alterations you're playing. This will open your ears to a whole new way of hearing things.

TRACK 9

44

C minor triad

D♭ minor triad

E♭ minor triad

F♯ minor triad

G minor triad

A minor triad

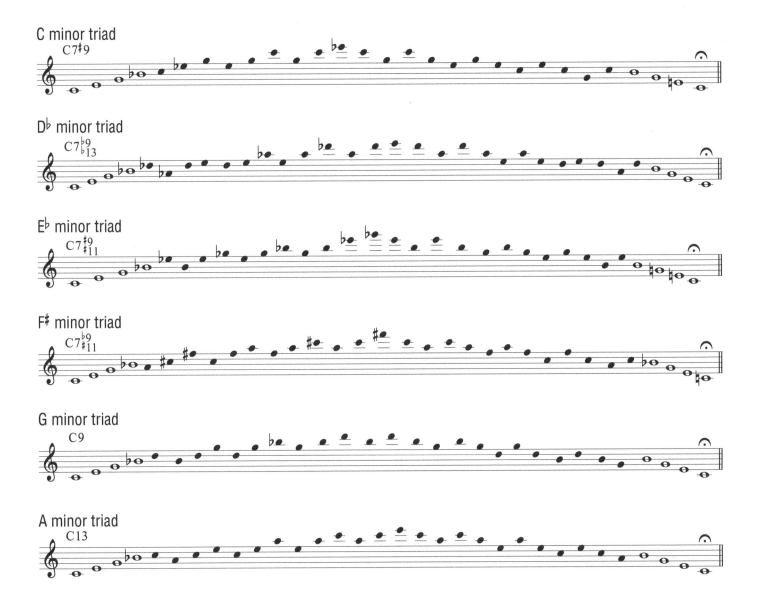

# Tritone Substitutions

*Idea #*

20

As you become fluent in the diatonic approach to improvisation, you'll want to experiment with chord substitutions to add chromaticism and tension and make your phrases more interesting. One of the more common chord substitutions is known as the tritone sub. The first example illustrates that two dominant seventh chords a tritone away from each other contain the same third and seventh notes. Both of these chords want to resolve to the tonic. Each note in the tritone substitution is just a half step away from the chord tones of the tonic, with one exception—the seventh.

The tritone sub works best when the V chord is resolving to a chord a fifth away. When using this substitution, keep it simple—the chord tones from the tritone sub work best. Using other notes from the scale or altering the extensions of the substitute chord will be counterproductive. Practice Examples A through G with track 3. Examples F and G illustrate how the relative IIm7 of the tritone substitution can also be incorporated.

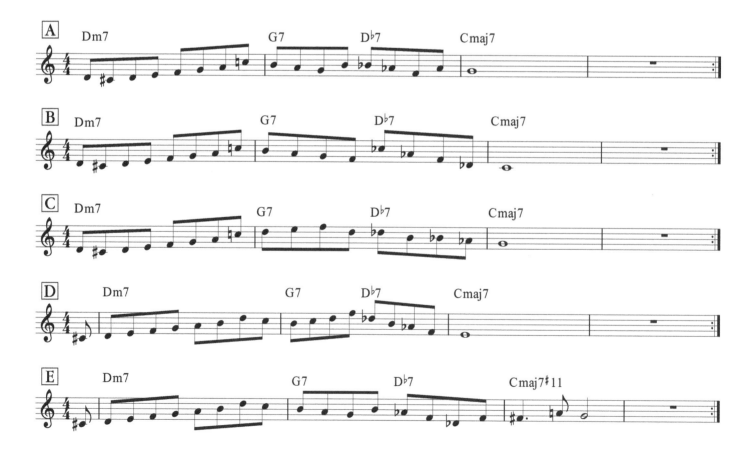

These exercises demonstrate additional ways of using the tritone sub. These substitutions can be played over the original II–V–I progression without the accompaniment changing to the new progression.

At first, it may be difficult to incorporate the substitutions into your playing. Allow your ear to get used to the new sounds. It's an acquired taste. As your ear adjusts to the dissonances, you'll begin to notice the substitutions in the playing of others, and gradually they will become a part of your jazz vocabulary.

# The Passing Diminished

*Idea #*21

When a minor seventh chord is sustained for a measure or more, you can alternate it with the diminished chord a half step down to add harmonic variety. Play the examples here in all keys, making sure to transpose by ear. Then create your own patterns.

# *Pentatonics*

*Idea #*

During the late fifties, jazz musicians started to stretch the harmonic, melodic, and rhythmic boundaries of bebop in an attempt to find a new sound. The five-note pentatonic scale became a popular melodic device because of its open sound and its ability to be inverted several ways to create interesting tonality. John Coltrane, Wayne Shorter, David Liebman, and Jerry Bergonzi are just a few of the saxophonists who frequently base their improvisations on pentatonic scales.

The pentatonic scale is a major scale without the fourth and seventh degrees. By eliminating the half steps, you have a scale without the tension notes (or notes that need to resolve).

**C Major Pentatonic**

There are many ways to shape the pentatonic scales. Here is a chart of some of the possibilities. By building pentatonic scales off various degrees of the chord, you can create sounds ranging from the very "inside" simplistic sound of the basic triad, to the tension sound of the major seventh, to the "outside" sound of the ♯11th.

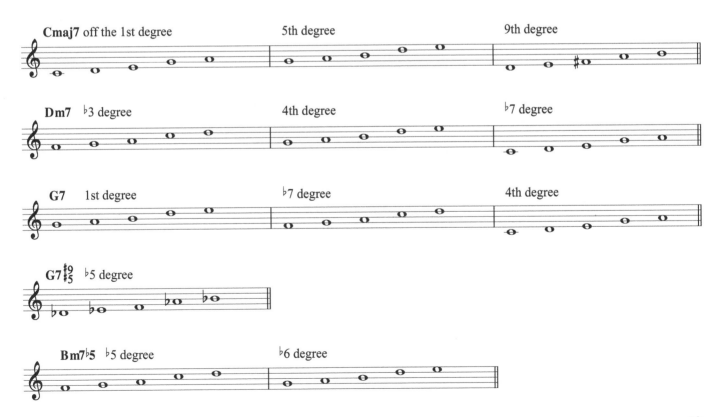

After learning to play the pentatonic scale in every key, begin to work on these patterns.

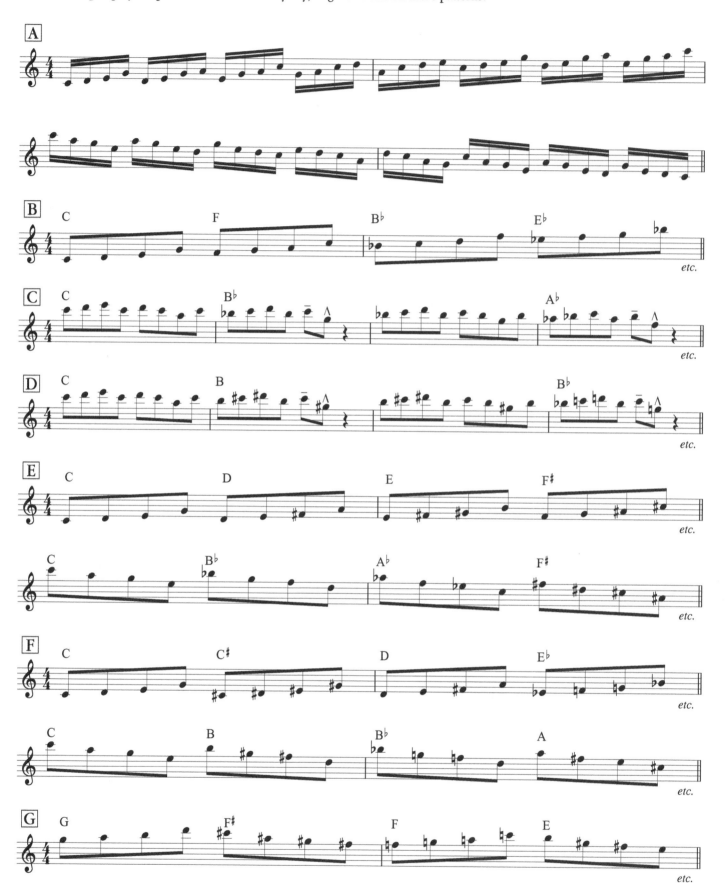

The next patterns are to be played with the major seventh chord track (track 10), so you can
hear how the different pentatonic scales sound against major chords.

**TRACK 10**

**Major Pentatonics**

These patterns are to be played with the minor chord track (track 11). As you can see, the possibilities are endless, so have fun creating your own pentatonic licks.

**Minor Pentatonics**

TRACK 11

# Jazz Legato Tonguing

*Idea #* 23

When you're playing a fast jazz piece it's essential to phrase properly. Tonguing every note is impractical and would sound stiff. It's best to tongue certain notes and slur by others, so some notes are not definite but ghosted or de-emphasized. This kind of jazz legato tonguing will allow you to play fast swinging phrases.

Important: For each of the following exercises, keep the tip of your tongue anchored behind your bottom teeth. Now use the thicker part of your tongue to lightly touch against the reed slightly in from the tip. Think the syllable *dooooo*.

In our first example, make each note legato with no space between the notes. Using a metronome, begin slowly (between 42 and 60 beats per minute). Try to achieve a uniform legato attack. Play chromatically through the range of your horn.

TRACK 12

Example B employs the bebop Mixolydian scale. Set the metronome on 2 and 4 between 44 and 66 b.p.m. Put a slight accent on the tongued notes. Strive for a nice swinging feel.

Example C is similar to Example B but is based on the diminished scale. Work toward being able to play this exercise starting on every note.

# Developing a Swing Feel

## Idea #

It's been said that the Count Basie Orchestra could swing playing just one note. In a group situation, swing—giving the music a fluid feel against a steady pulse—depends on all the musicians coming to an agreement on how to phrase the rhythmic aspects of the music. Individually, each person's concept of swing is as identifiable and unique as his or her sound.

Swing is one of the hardest concepts to master. You can sit in a practice room for hours learning all your scales and chords and creating exercises to develop your ear, but how do you learn to play phrases in a swinging style? The first step is to listen. Choose a medium swing tune by a favorite sax player and listen to it until you're able to sing along with the solo note for note, making up your own syllables to convey all the nuances of the solo. Note how the eighth notes are swung. The underlying pulse is based on triplets, with the first two notes of the triplet tied together. Now pick up your horn and try to reproduce the solo. This is the best way to really learn the ins and outs of rhythmic interpretation.

Once you start to get comfortable with the jazz legato tonguing exercises in Idea #23, begin playing the brief excerpts I've included here. Set the metronome on 2 and 4. I've included the articulations and accents to help you achieve a good swing feel. Accenting and de-emphasizing (ghosting or swallowing) certain notes will help lead to amazing phrasing.

Listening to bebop tunes will help teach you to think in terms of eighth notes as the basic pulse. Learn as many of these tunes as you can either directly from the recordings or from fake books.

# Energizing Your Lines

*Idea #*

25

Have you ever noticed how some solos sound as though they are meandering while others possess a sense of logic and a feeling of movement? Play Examples A and B below back to back a few times. Notice how Example B seems to swing a little harder and sounds more fluid. This is because I've displaced the first eighth note by half a beat. By beginning a phrase on an upbeat and ending a phrase on a strong beat (beat 1 or 3), you give the line direction and movement. This allows the listener to hear where the phrases are going. If a solo lacks direction and sounds like noodling, it's probably because the strong tones of the scale (root, third, fifth, and seventh) and the strong beats are not in sync.

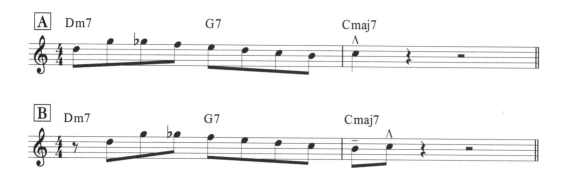

The following exercises are based on playing the Mixolydian scale over a II–V–I progression. The strong tones and strong beats are aligned in the phrases. Play these exercises with track 3. Example C is based on the root and third. Example D is based on the third and fifth. Example E is based on the fifth and seventh. Examples F and G are combinations.

As you can see, these phrases start to take on the contour of many bebop lines. Work on trying to hear ahead of where you are playing. This will also help give your phrases momentum. As you become familiar with these exercises, your ear should pull you into the next chord.

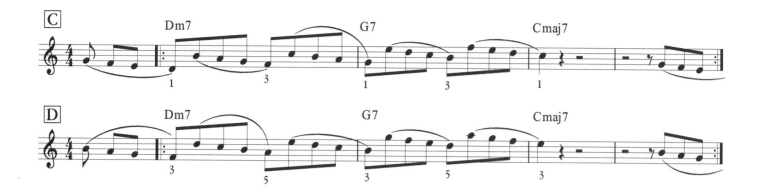

# Manipulating Time

*Idea #*

Developing a strong sense of time will enhance your phrasing and make your playing more expressive. The first step is to realize that the beat is a space and not a point in time. Imagine that the beat looks like this:

There are basically three ways to approach where to place your beat. Playing in time or "in the pocket" would be placing your downbeat right in the middle (A). If you were to place the pulse on the front part of the beat, that's referred to as playing on "top" of the time (B). If you lean toward the back side of the beat, that's "laying back" (C). If it sounds like you're rushing or dragging, that means you're overdoing it (D or E). Stretching and compressing the beat for musical effect is what we're striving for.

Naturally, the slower pace of ballads and blues numbers give more freedom and ways to manipulate time. Your choice of where to place the beat is as unique and personal as your tone. Lester Young and Gene Ammons played more on the back side of the beat, while Sonny Stitt and Don Byas generally phrased on top of the beat. But you don't want to play exclusively one way; good improvisers manipulate time and play all over the beat depending on the musical situation and what they are trying to express.

The following exercises are designed to get you comfortable with placing notes within the beat. Set your metronome on beats 2 and 4. Imagine this as a drummer's high hat. Now play the first exercise—on the beat. After repeating this until you're at ease with the time, try pushing ahead to the front of the beat. Be careful not to push too far and turn the beat around. Once you've established playing on top of the beat, slide back to the middle and repeat several times. Then pull back until you're consistently playing on the back side of the beat. Once you get used to the feel of manipulating the time, begin to expand the exercises to full scales or other patterns found in this book. After working with this concept for a while, you should begin to feel control of time and phrasing.

# Three Against Four

*Idea #*

27

In this book I focus much attention on developing and expanding the vocabulary of harmony and melody. In addition to good note choices, a good improviser must be able to shift in and out of meter, creating rhythmic ambiguity. The musicians in Miles Davis' quintet of the sixties (Herbie Hancock on piano, Tony Williams on drums, Ron Carter on bass, and either George Coleman or Wayne Shorter on sax) were masters of rhythmic innovation. The band was able to make the music sound fresh through their use of polyrhythms and phrasing over the bar line.

Examples A and B use a simple scale passage. You create metric displacement by shifting the accents, thereby changing the perception of where the downbeat occurs. The first step in doing this is knowing where you are in the measure at all times. Put the metronome on beats 2 and 4 at a slow tempo. Accent every third beat. In these examples, the accents fall on beat 3 in the first measure, beat 2 in the second measure, and beats 1 and 4 in the third measure. Then the cycle begins again. Play in different keys and try your own patterns. Technique is not the emphasis here. It's the feeling of playing three against four.

Example C uses a different kind of accent, called a durational accent. Note that the duration of the long notes on beats 2 and 4 create a shift in the pulse away from the downbeats, creating the illusion of playing three against four. In Example D, three against four is created by using a repeated three-note pattern. Example E is much like Examples A and B, accenting every third beat, this time beginning on beat 2.

# Rhythmic Displacement

*Idea #* 28

As the name implies, rhythmic displacement means shifting where a repeating rhythm falls in the measure by the use of a rest. It can be an eighth rest, quarter rest, or dotted quarter rest.

In the first example, two quarter notes are followed by an eighth rest. The rest displaces the next two quarter notes to the **and** of beats 3 **and** four **and**. The displacement by an eighth rest continues until the cycle is completed. Modern jazz and commercial music are filled with the use of this device.

Play the next example along with the funk track (track 26), then experiment with your own examples.

# Chromatic Scales in Cycle

*Idea #*

29

This is a chromatic exercise based on the cycle of fourths. The idea is to build technique while working on phrasing over the bar line. Instead of playing phrases built on eight-note or sixteen-note groupings, these phrases are played in groups of twelve , twenty-four, or thirty-six notes. Play G to G and then C to C chromatically, without a pause between starting points, so that it is like one thought or sentence. Practice slowly and evenly with the metronome. As you build up speed, extend the phrase to three or four groups—for example, G to G, C to C, and F to F—or as many as you can in one breath. Take a deep breath, then continue where you left off (B♭ to B♭, E♭ to E♭, etc.). As you practice this, keep switching octaves when possible to work on the entire range of the horn.

TRACK 13

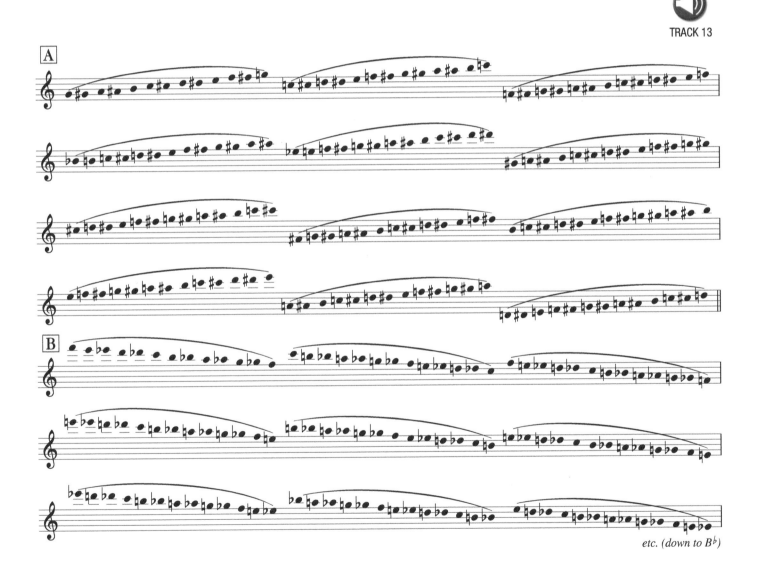

*etc. (down to B♭)*

# Challenge Tempo

*Idea #*

Let's look at a systematic approach for mastering challenging musical passages.

- **Step 1**

  Establish a reference tempo—a tempo at which you can comfortably read through the passage with a great deal of accuracy. Find this tempo on the metronome.

- **Step 2**

  Now try a challenge tempo. Your first challenge tempo is one metronome marking higher than your reference tempo. Play your challenge tempo, then alternate with your reference tempo. When you've become accurate with your challenge tempo—you can play the passage three times in a row without a mistake—increase the challenge tempo one more notch. Keep repeating this procedure until you reach your target tempo.

As you work through this process, isolate problem areas. If there's a particular spot that keeps you from achieving your challenge tempo, break it down and work on it by isolating the problem note and the preceding note. Play the two slowly, placing each one on the beat. Now include the note after the problem note with the same rhythm. After a few successful attempts, still keeping the slow rhythm, enlarge the isolated area to include a few more notes. When you feel comfortable with that, try the entire measure with the dotted-eighth-note rhythm. Now try to reach your challenge tempo.

# Creating Melodies

*Idea #*

"John Coltrane could play a melody," vocalist Freddy Cole told John McDonough in the July 2001 issue of *Downbeat*. "John Coltrane knew the whole thing inside out before he got to do what he did. Students have to go and listen to these other things. Trouble is they want to start where Coltrane ended. But they don't realize that Coltrane came from the melody. That's true of all the great instrumentalists—Louis Armstrong, Miles Davis, Dizzy—they knew the song. The root to artistry is through the melody."

Spontaneous melodic invention is the true essence of improvisation. Every soloist must learn to create original melodies and communicate them in the most direct way possible. The following are some of the elements to good melody writing.

1.  Keep a proper balance of diatonic movement and leaps. Stepwise motion is the norm, while skips are added for variety and intensity and to outline a chord. Remember, most melodies were written to be sung. After a wide skip, turn in the other direction.

2.  After two skips in the same direction, reverse and go in the opposite direction, as in this example.

3.  The melody should have direction. Aim toward a climax point. Don't noodle. If your line keeps circling around a certain pitch or stays confined to a narrow range, it will lose its effectiveness. Building to one spot and then another will give your melody a sense of momentum. Once you reach the climax, descend gradually to a point of less intensity or release. Here's an example.

4.  Don't let your phrases end on the same note each time. Any tone that keeps being repeated will bog down your phrase. Try to achieve a question-and-answer effect over an eight-measure phrase. This will give your melody a conversational feel. This example doesn't sound like a complete statement until it's resolved in measure 8.

5. Keep a proper balance between introducing new material and repeating old material. If every phrase is new, there won't be enough continuity. Listeners unconsciously predict where the phrase is going; if it's too predictable they will be bored, but if it's too unpredictable you'll also lose them.

6. Varying the length of the phrases when improvising will keep the listener off balance. Usually the length of the phrase is governed by the idea itself. Shorter melodic phrases at the beginning of the solo are more conducive to development.

7. To become a more melodic player, play melodies. As simple as that sounds, it's often overlooked. Take a fake book and spend time each day playing melodies. If you know the song, close the book and play it by ear. If it's a song you aren't familiar with, play it exactly as written the first time through. As you become more acquainted with the new melody, begin to use the techniques discussed in Idea #32 to arrive at your own interpretation of the tune.

   Playing with a vocalist will also help develop your melodic sense. Take a vocal version of a favorite standard and learn it note for note, including all the singer's nuances, and reproduce it on your horn.

8. How do you get from playing a string of pitches into developing a cohesive melodic phrase? Start with a simple idea or motif and expand upon it. You can repeat the melodic idea exactly:

Transpose it to a higher pitch:

Transpose it to a lower pitch:

Change some of the intervals:

Or use sequencing: take the original motif and move the pitches but keep the same intervallic relationships. Used properly, this helps create cohesion and balance.

# Melodic Embellishment

*Idea #*

In section A of the music below, you'll find a melody written in the style typical of a fake book or lead sheet. It's an easy-to-read basic sketch of the song, usually written in simple rhythms to accommodate all levels of musicianship. It's up to the player to interpret the melody. Here are a few common devices.

**Anticipation** (*Ant.*):     anticipating the melody note by half a beat.

**Delayed attack** (*D.A.*):   delaying the attack of the melody note by half a beat.

**Augmentation** (*Aug.*):     enlarging a melodic phrase by using auxiliary pitches.

**Diminution** (*Dim.*):       shortening a melodic phrase.

In sections B and C we interpret the same melody using these melodic embellishment techniques. (I've identified the different techniques underneath the melody.) Play this piece as written along with track 14. Then try creating your own melodic embellishments.

TRACK 14

# Contour Lines

*Idea #*

These exercises are designed to help you develop linear (scalewise) melodic lines while moving through chord changes. Each exercise uses the Mixolydian mode. Example A is built on a cycle-of-fourths chord progression: by moving the root of each chord in fourths, you cycle through all twelve keys. This important cycle is the basis of many jazz tunes. Note that the scales move stepwise using the rhythm of eighth notes. At the point of each chord change, move into the new chord using either a half step or whole step. It is important to give your lines some contour, so try to build your scales in a roller-coaster shape using the entire range of your horn. Pick a tempo that will enable you to move from one chord to the next without pausing.

Examples B and C use dominant chords moving down in whole steps. Example D uses dominant chords moving up in half steps, while Example E uses dominant seventh chords moving down in half steps. Once you feel comfortable with the written exercise, try starting on another chord tone. Remember to look and hear ahead and keep your lines running smoothly through the chords.

TRACK 15

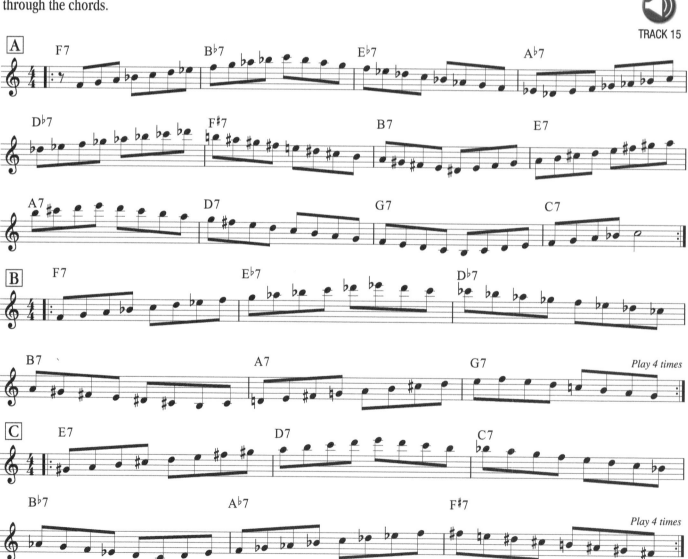

The same exercises can be done using the Dorian scale.

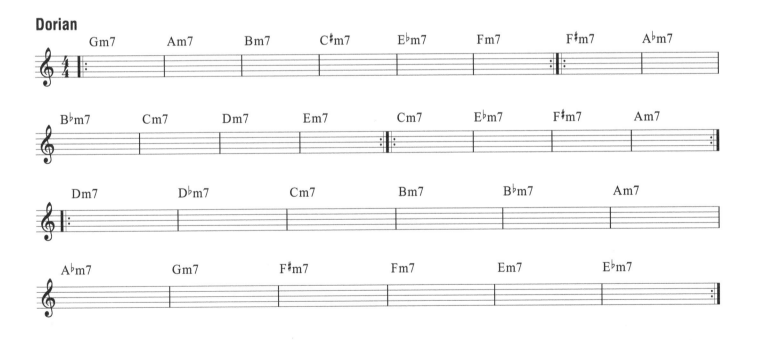

# The Blues Scale

*Idea #*

3 4

The blues scale is a six-note scale made up of the root, ♭3, 4, ♭5, 5, and ♭7. The ♭3 and ♭5 give it its characteristic bluesy sound. The beauty of this scale is that you can use one scale for the entire 12-bar blues.

*G Blues Scale*

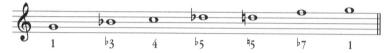

The following is a hybrid blues scale that adds a major third. The major third is not a substitute for the minor third; they are used together. The minor third often precedes the major third to create a bluesy sound.

*Hybrid Blues Scale*

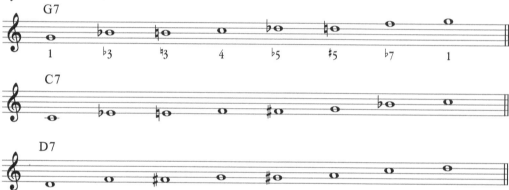

Before beginning this exercise, pan the saxophone from the audio track. Then, play the head one time followed by your own blues solo using the blues scale. After a few passes, when you feel comfortable, try incorporating the hybrid scales. Remember, the blues is based on feeling, so try to use some inflections to give the music more impact.

TRACK 16

# Blues Guide-Tone Line

*Idea #*

A guide-tone line is based on the third or seventh note of the chord that weaves its way through the progression, moving by a half step or whole step at each chord change. (The third and the seventh are the most important notes of each chord because they give each chord its identity.) Listen to the blues progression on track 16; the second and third choruses demonstrate the guide-tone line. Now stop the track and play these guide-tone lines—first the top line, then the bottom line. By sounding the most important notes in each chord, you should be able to hear the blues progression by just playing the single-note line.

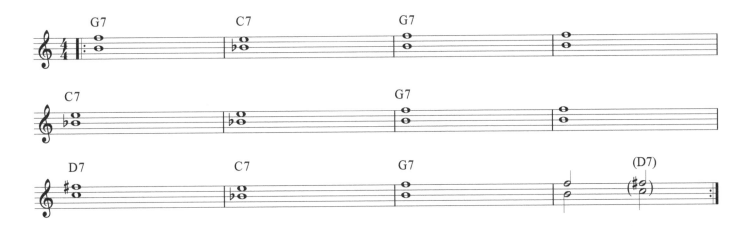

Now look at the following solo, which is based on starting a line off the third of each chord change. Play the written solo with track 16, then try creating your own. At first, you may need to write the solo out, but work toward being able to do it on the fly. Then go through this progression building a solo starting each chord change on the seventh.

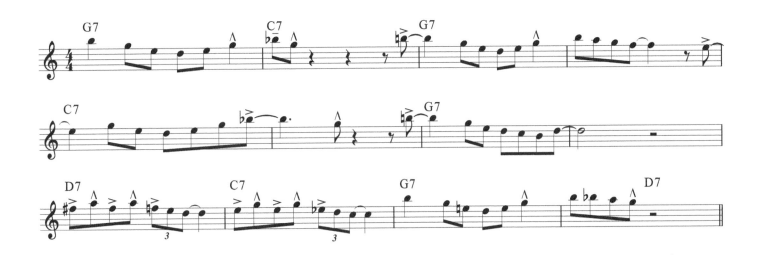

The next solo uses a combination of the two guide-tone lines, with the third or seventh being played at every chord change.

# Melodies from the Blues Scale

*Idea #* 36

In this exercise we'll set a mood and create melodies using the six notes of the F$\sharp$ blues scale. Take your time; there is no pulse. Simply play and rearrange the notes in the scale to create bluesy melodies. Note the active tones (the ones that feel like they need to resolve) and the rest tones (the notes that a phrase can end on). After trying this a few times, compare your results to the audio track.

TRACK 17

# Building a Solo

## Idea #

*37*

Every good solo tells a story. It should have a beginning, build interest toward a climax, and then wind its way back down to the conclusion. The following five-chorus blues solo demonstrates these points. The solo begins in a relaxed manner in the low to middle range of the sax. Starting at an easy volume and with short phrases gives you plenty room to build. Each chorus gets a little busier and more harmonically complex while the notes steadily climb up the horn, reaching a climax in the first two measures of the last chorus.

The solo begins mainly with chord tones, establishing a major tonality. As it progresses, more of the ♭3 and ♭5 blues notes come into play, and the phrases lengthen, giving the listener the sense of digging in. After the solo climaxes, it winds back down using some inventive chord substitutions.

It's important before you begin your solo to have in mind how many choruses you're going to take, so you can pace yourself accordingly. Always try for a strong opening statement. This will get you on solid footing and give you something to build on.

TRACK 18

# Arpeggiating Chords in a Progression

*Idea #*38

A valuable first step when learning a new song is to play the arpeggios to the progression. This helps you to become familiar with the harmonic structure of the song and hear how the chords work together.

Work slowly through the whole tune/progression playing the arpeggios to the chords as in the example below:

Example A: root position

Example B: voice leading (resolving to the next nearest chord tone)

Example C: reverse movement (down and up instead of up and down)

Example D: altering each dominant chord with a ♭9 that has a V–I relationship

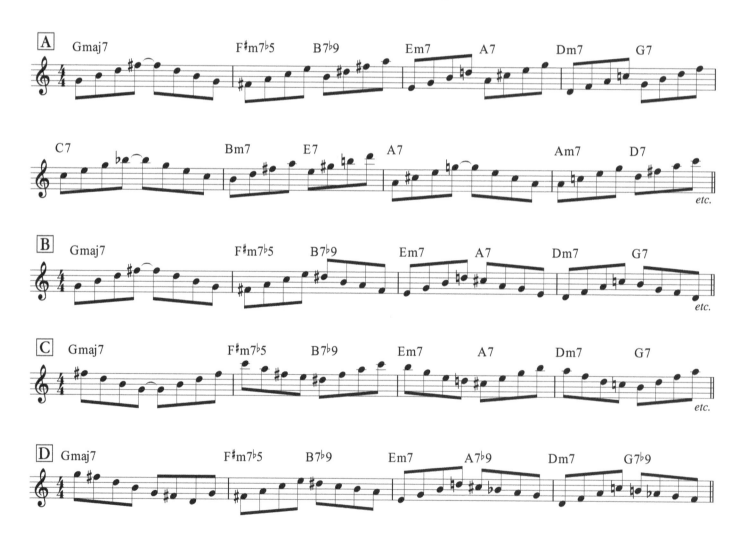

Write out these arpeggios, if you need to, as you work through your song.

The following étude is based on playing through an entire progression using only chord tones. The second time through, ♯9 and ♭9 are used on the dominant chords whenever possible. Play along with the recording, then try writing out your own solo. Once you feel comfortable with the changes, practice improvising your own solo.

TRACK 19

# Chord Scales

*Idea #*

The chord-scale approach is based on the idea that for every chord there's a corresponding scale. A chord scale contains not only chord tones but the tensions of that chord, so it can help you find the more colorful melody notes. Chord scales are also useful for learning new tunes.

The following example demonstrates which scale is applied to each chord in a progression based on a standard jazz tune. Major, Dorian, and Mixolydian scales are used here. Listen to how the nonchord tones fit with the chords.

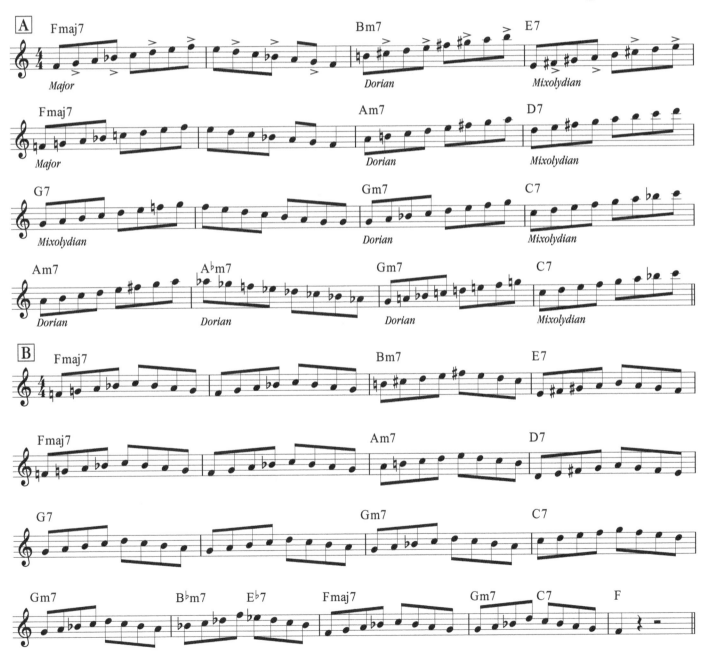

Now try this chord-scale étude. Practice it with the track, with or without the sax part. In the second chorus, the étude starts to alter some of the dominant seventh chords, providing more tension and color tones. Analyze the alterations and make a mental note of the ones that you like, so you can include them in your solos. Practice writing out your own solos.

To improve your phrasing and create a sense of momentum, make a conscious effort to begin your phrases on upbeats. Practice getting your lines to flow into the next chord, and always remember to shape your lines so they have direction and don't sound mechanical. When you feel comfortable playing your written-out études, try applying the above techniques to your own improvised solo.

TRACK 20

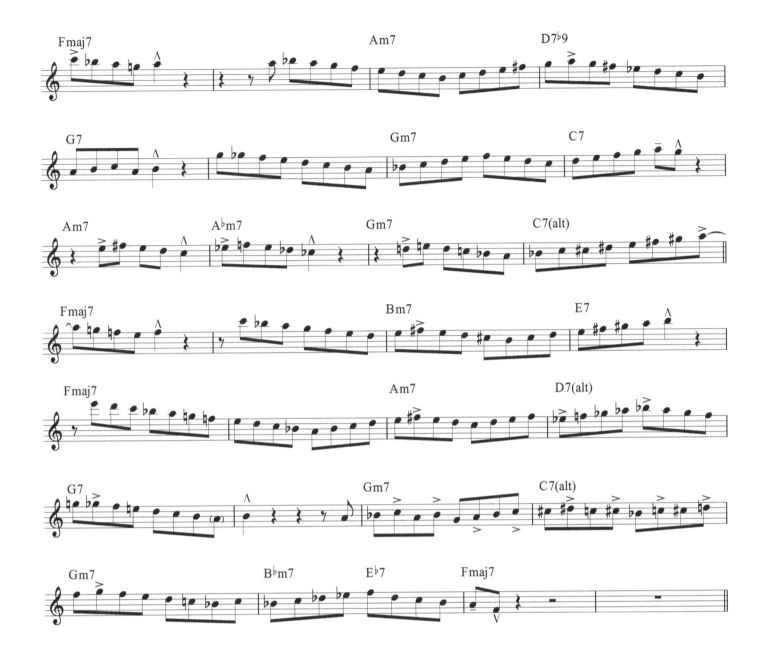

# Horizontal and Vertical Approaches

*Idea #*

There are two basic ways to negotiate chord changes—a horizontal approach or a vertical approach. In a horizontal approach, the emphasis is on playing in a linear or scalewise fashion. Lester Young and Dexter Gordon are proponents of this style. In a vertical approach the improvisation is based on arpeggiating the chord changes—Coleman Hawkins and Sonny Rollins are closely identified with this style. Good solos are often made up of elements from both approaches.

The following example, a blues in C, incorporates both approaches. The first two choruses use the horizontal approach, while the last two employ the vertical style.

TRACK 21

# Making Patterns Musical

## Idea #41

How can you make sequenced patterns sound like music rather than simply exercises? One way to add the human element is repeating certain notes and giving the rhythm a more elastic feel. This will make the patterns breathe and sound fresh, as you can see in this example.

TRACK 22

# Soloing in a Limited Range

*Idea #*

Confining the melody of a solo to a limited range allows the improviser to focus more attention on the note choices. The usual resolutions from chord to chord may not be available within the limited range, forcing you to find new ways to play through the changes. This will also aid in training your ear to hear and get inside the chord changes. Work on trying to hear ahead of where you are, moving into the next chord.

The following solo is three choruses long, with the first two choruses limited to the range of a sixth. The first chorus is confined to the notes between D♭ and B♭. The second chorus (B) is within the range of B to G♯. The final chorus (C) is confined to the range of a fifth—A to E. After playing the written solo a few times with the recording, remove the sax from the track and try playing your own solo, keeping within the range of a major sixth. As you become more familiar with the progression, restrict the range to a fifth or a fourth. Restrictions, when used appropriately in the practice room, will actually expand rather than limit your ideas.

TRACK 23

# Rhythm Changes

## Idea #

Up until the forties, the jazz repertoire was based on popular songs and blues numbers. During the bebop era, jazz musicians began creating new melodies and using chord substitutions within the framework of existing standard tunes. Countless songs were based on George and Ira Gershwin's "I Got Rhythm," including "Moose the Mooche" (Charlie Parker), "Lester Leaps In" (Lester Young), "Oleo" (Sonny Rollins), "Rhythm-a-ning" (Thelonious Monk), and the Flintstones' TV theme. This is an important chord progression to know, because of the large number of tunes based on it.

"I Got Rhythm" is a thirty-two-measure AABA composition featuring a tonic-based progression for the first sixteen measures. For the bridge, the song moves up a major third and, using the cycle of fourths, works its way back to the tonic.

The first two choruses of the solo below are based on the standard "rhythm changes." The next two choruses use a variety of chord substitutions to bring a more modern approach. After learning the solo, try playing the last two choruses over the rhythm section playing the first two choruses. This allows you to play "outside" by superimposing one set of chords over another.

TRACK 24

# Playing in a Key Center

*Idea #*

For most of this book, the focus has been on the ins and outs of "making all the changes." Now let's take a look at the big picture. Analyzing the chord progression in the following example, we find that the first four measures are all chords that can be found in the key of C. The next four measures are diatonic to A minor, C major's relative minor. In fact, each chord in the first sixteen measures, with the exception of E7, can be negotiated by using the C major scale. The only note in E7 that doesn't fit is the third, G#, so we need to avoid the G# and sound some of the other chord tones on the E7. Measures 11 and 12 are a series of passing chords leading to F major. By using careful manipulation, we can make it through this section by still playing the C major scale. (Note: in the second chorus, the passing chords are dealt with by laying out.)

Even though this piece is in A minor, the entire two choruses are played in the relative major, C. By thinking C major all the way through the piece, you will have a nice linear framework to work in as well as interesting tension notes on some of the chords.

It's easy to get hung up on being too analytical/complicated in an improvisation and play all the hip scales over every chord. Always keep the big picture in mind instead of thinking each chord individually. The simplest approach can often give the most interesting results.

TRACK 25

# *One-Chord Vamps*

While soloing over a composition with many chord changes can be difficult, playing an interesting solo over one chord presents a different sort of challenge. The first step is to have some sort of plan formulated as to the length of the solo. In the opening statement, play a short phrase or motif that you can easily repeat at various times to give your solo an overall structure as well as providing material to build from. To create interest in the development stage, try superimposing other modes or scales, implying other tonal centers. Chords or scales a whole step, half step, minor or major third, or tritone away work best.

Here are some ideas for playing over a Dm vamp. Example A uses Dm and Fm, while Example B uses D and B♭7. Example C uses Dm and A♭7, Example D uses Dm and E♭m, and Example E runs through several keys—B♭, A♭, and F.

TRACK 26

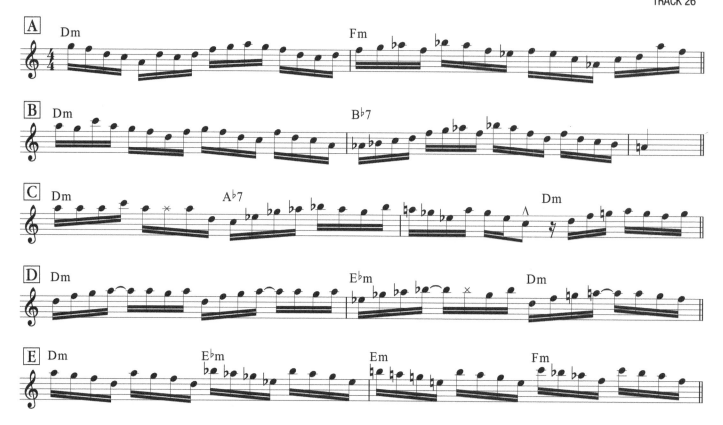

Practice this with the one-chord vamp track on the recording. Begin playing the D minor pentatonic scale, establishing the sound of the tonic. Concentrate on playing with a strong rhythmic pulse, then superimpose one of the other scales or chords above, starting with short forays into the new key and then quickly returning to home base. As you get accustomed to the sound, become more adventurous in the length of your phrases in the new keys. Try running through several keys before returning to the original key. Another technique that will add tension and excitement to one-chord solos is the use of sequences. Play a series of notes in one key, then transpose the same series of notes up or down a half step or whole step, as in Example E.

# Neighboring Tones

*Idea #*

Jazz instrumentalists often incorporate neighboring tones in their phrases to create tension and
release. Practice these exercises in all twelve keys using a variety of articulations.

# Approach Notes

*Idea #* 47

A device often used by jazz players to add chromaticism to their solos is to approach a chord tone by a half step above or below. In this étude, we begin by using the single-note half-step approach, then expand the idea to include a double chromatic approach—using two notes, one a half step above and one a half step below the target note. The idea continues to expand throughout the étude to the point of approaching each target note chromatically from a fourth away. To improve your phrasing, practice with a metronome and observe all articulation markings.

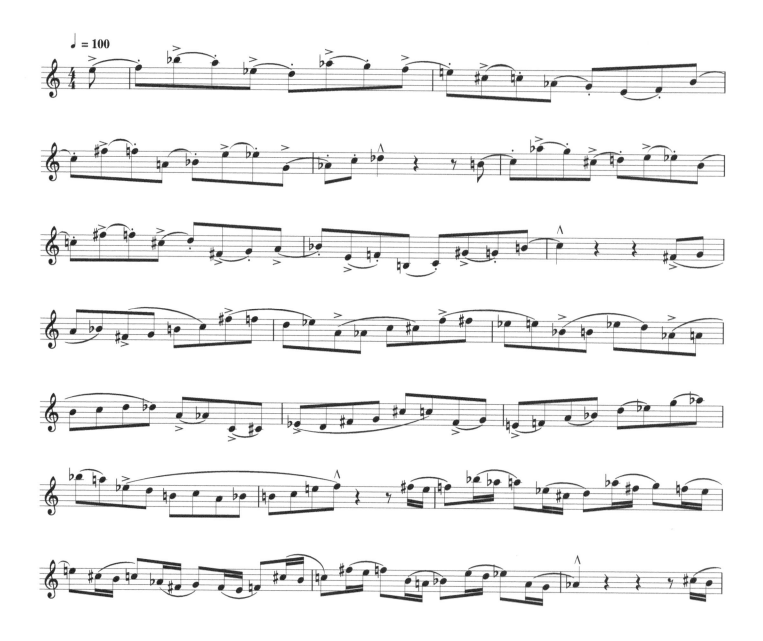

# Developing a Motif

One way to develop your ideas is to build from one little cell or motif. For example, take the basic major pattern (1–2–3–5 on major and dominant chords and 3–4–5–7 on minor chords) and see how many ways it can be twisted around to form new patterns. John Coltrane's approach to playing his composition "Giant Steps" is a good example of this approach.

Example A shows the basic major pattern motif ascending over the chord progression. Example B is the same motif reversed (5–3–2–1) over the same chord changes. Examples C and D alternate direction (C is up/down, D is down/up). Example E combines the above examples and begins to take on the characteristics of an improvised line.

Example F follows the same ascending pattern as Example A, but the basic motif is now minor (5–6–7–9 on minor and dominant chords, 6–7–1–3 on major chords). Example G follows the same descending pattern as Example B, but in the minor. Examples H through J combine the major and minor patterns used previously over the same progression. The possibilities for melodic ideas all based on one four-note motif are limitless.

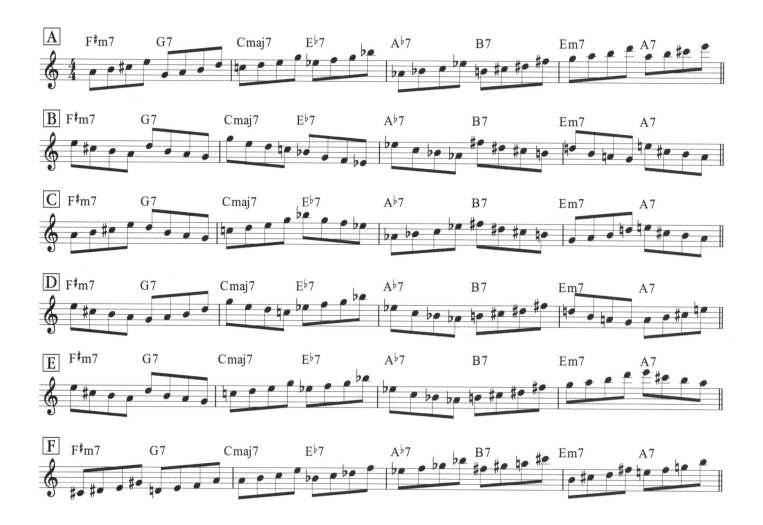

# Flexible Embouchure

## Idea #

In order to produce a resonant sound on the saxophone, it's important to allow the reed to vibrate freely. When attaching the ligature, make sure that the screws aren't constricting the vibrations of the reed. If you use a ligature with two screws, tighten the bottom one fully but make sure the top one is just snug. If you use a ligature with one screw, tighten it just enough to keep the reed in place. Your lips should be like a rubber band around the mouthpiece—even pressure all the way around. The bottom lip acts like a cushion tucked over the teeth. Just place the mouthpiece and reed on the bottom lip. That will provide enough of a cushion. A little flesh should show. Don't curl your lip in. If your lip is curled in too far, you'll be restricting the vibration of the reed, producing a dull, nonresonant sound and, eventually, intonation problems. The top lip should be over the teeth and resting on the mouthpiece. Clamping will reduce flexibility. The corners of your mouth should be pulled back into a slight smile.

Here are a couple of good exercises to help develop the muscles in the embouchure.

1.  Move the smile muscles back and forth by repeating the sounds "tuu-eee, tuu-eee," exaggerating the mouth movement.

2.  Place the tongue in the E position, as in saying the word eel. Now make a chewing motion in the corners of the mouth. Limit the jaw motion. Keep doing this until you begin to feel a slight burning sensation in the corners of your mouth.

The most resonant tone produces lots of overtones. Here is an overtone exercise I got from master saxophone instructor Joe Allard. The sax, like the brass instruments, is capable of producing a series of overtones off of the low fingerings of the horn. This exercise will help you gain control and flexibility in your embouchure, forcing you to adjust your throat and larynx and open up your sound. Play slowly, fingering the low notes but producing the pitches written on the top line. The lower overtones are produced with an "aaah" sound. The higher you go, it's more like an "eee" sound. This exercise will help you achieve an even sound from the bottom to the top of the horn, in addition to giving your sound a core and an intensity. If you play too loud or make the note too big, you will destroy the core. The core is what makes your sound project.

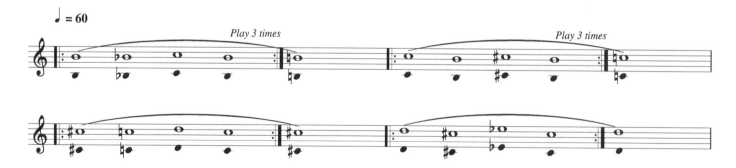

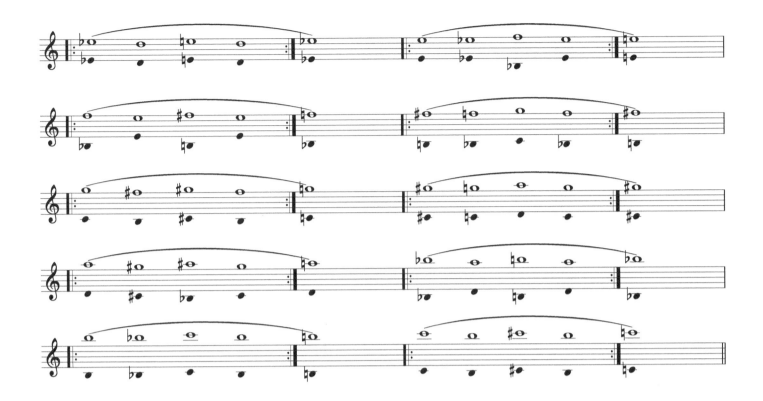

Here's another exercise to help you to slur wide intervals and to promote flexibility in your embouchure. Keep your throat open and drop your jaw slightly as you play through the exercise.

In this exercise, you move from a subtone to a regular tone. Start each note with a whisper, then crescendo, then fade back to a whisper. For a subtone you need to drop the jaw and flex your bottom lip slightly. Support the reed by using the muscles of the bottom lip rather than the teeth underneath your lip. As the bottom lip rolls out a bit, it becomes more flexed. To move from a subtone to a regular tone, start with the lip in the flexed position and slowly roll the lip back over the teeth. Learning to control this will take a bit of practice, but it will help to strengthen your embouchure and develop more colors for your tonal palate.

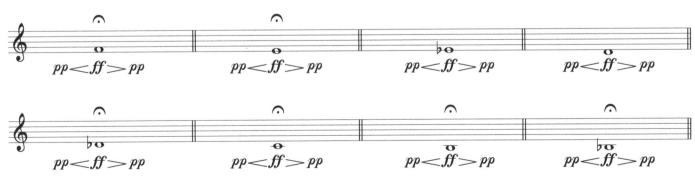

# *Finding Your Voice*

In the movie *'Round Midnight,* the lead character played by sax great Dexter Gordon says, "You don't just go out and pick a style off a tree. One day, the tree is inside of you growing naturally." How do you find that tree? We all steal a little bit from our musical heroes and blend all of our influences to form our own style. It's natural to be attracted to the tone of specific sax players while liking the musical ideas of others. Knowing the history of the instrument and listening to all the great players past and present will help you find your own sound. Stan Getz was certainly influenced by Lester Young, but what Getz arrived at was uniquely his own voice. A good exercise is to transcribe the solos of other musicians—not just sax players—and capture every nuance, then translate their ideas into your own.

Another exercise that I find helpful is attempting to capture another musician's essence by playing in his or her style. I don't copy solos note for note but try to evoke that musician's musical spirit and style by mentally identifying the things that make them distinctive or unique. For example, Sonny Rollins has a muscular sound, is an aggressive player, and plays large leaps, rhythmically in and out of time. Lester Young has a light, airy tone and plays long lines with deceptive resolutions. Gene Ammons has a full-bodied tone deeply rooted in blues and plays lazy, behind-the-beat phrasing. Pinpointing all these idiosyncratic elements in other players is essential in developing your own voice.

Having a knowledge of a wide variety of musical idioms will have another important influence on your style. The more styles of music you listen to—classical, Latin, Eastern European, funk, avant-garde, pop, etc.—the more "vocabulary" you have to draw upon in creating your own distinctive voice.

# About the Author

Nominated in 1999 and 2000 for the Nashville Music Awards' Miscellaneous Wind Instrumentalist of the Year, saxophonist Dennis Taylor (tenor, alto, soprano, and baritone) has been playing the saxophone professionally for more than twenty-five years. He's toured and/or recorded with a wide variety of artists including Clarence "Gatemouth" Brown, Buckwheat Zydeco, Duke Robillard, Shelby Lynne, Eddy "the Chief" Clearwater, Robert Jr. Lockwood, "Mighty" Sam McClain, Sam Moore (Sam and Dave), Dan Penn, Jay McShann, Kenny Rogers, and John Hammond. Taylor has played on four Grammy-nominated albums and has appeared on *Austin City Limits, The Road*, the "Country Music Hall of Fame 25th Anniversary Celebration," *Texas Connection, ABC in Concert Country, American Music Shop,* and *Music City Tonight.*

## Acknowledgments

This book is dedicated to all the teachers who have inspired me and all the fabulous musicians I've played with over the years.

Special thanks go to my wife, Karen, for her constant support and encouragement and to my parents, Ad and Lois, for instilling in me the love of music and the belief that anything is possible.

## Musicians

Tenor saxophone: Dennis Taylor

Piano: Darryl Dybka

Bass: John Vogt

Drums: Chris Brown

Recorded at Three Little Pigs Studio, Nashville, Tennessee
Engineered, mixed, and mastered by Joe Funderburk